DISCOVERERS
AND
EXPLORERS

DISCOVERERS AND EXPLORERS

By

EDWARD R. SHAW

GYAN

Published by

Gyan Publishing House
5, Ansari Road
Daryaganj, New Delhi-110002
Phone: 011-47034999, 9811692060
E-mail: books@gyanbooks.com

Distribution Network
gyanbooks.com
India, USA, Canada, UK, Australia, France

ISBN : 978-81-212-6436-5 (PB)
First Published, 1900

2nd Impression 2022

Printed at: Gyan Press, Delhi.

DISCOVERERS AND EXPLORERS
Author: EDWARD R. SHAW

DISCOVERERS

AND

EXPLORERS

BY

EDWARD R. SHAW

1900

PREFACE.

THE practice of beginning the study of geography with the locality in which the pupil lives, in order that his first ideas of geographical conceptions may be gained from observation directed upon the real conditions existing about him, has been steadily gaining adherence during the past few years as a rational method of entering upon the study of geography.

After the pupil has finished an elementary study of the locality, he is ready to pass to an elementary consideration of the world as a whole, to get his first conception of the planet on which he lives. His knowledge of the forms of land and water, his knowledge of rain and wind, of heat and cold, as agents, and of the easily traced effects resulting from the interaction of these agents, have been acquired by observation and inference upon conditions actually at hand; in other words, his knowledge has been gained in a presentative manner.

His study of the world, however, must differ largely from this, and must be effected principally by representation. The globe in relief, therefore, presents to him his basic idea, and all his future study of the world will but expand and modify this idea, until at length, if the study is properly continued, the idea becomes exceedingly complex.

In passing from the geography of the locality to that of the world as a whole, the pupil is to deal broadly with the land masses and their general characteristics. The continents and oceans, their relative situations, form, and size, are then to be treated, but the treatment is always to be kept easily within the pupil's capabilities—the end being merely an elementary world-view.

During the time the pupil is acquiring this elementary knowledge of the world as a whole, certain facts of history may be interrelated with the geographical study.

According to the plan already suggested, it will be seen that the pupil is carried out from a study of the limited area of land and water about him to an idea of the world as a sphere, with its great distribution of land and water. In this transference he soon comes to perceive how small a part his hitherto known world forms of the great earth-sphere itself.

Something analogous to this transition on the part of the pupil to a larger view seems to be found in the history of the western nations of Europe. It is the gradual change in the conception of the world held during the fourteenth and fifteenth centuries to the enlarged conception of the world as a sphere which the remarkable discoveries and explorations of the fifteenth and sixteenth centuries brought about.

The analogy serves pedagogically to point out an interesting and valuable *interrelation* of certain facts of history with certain phases of geographical study.

This book has been prepared for the purpose of affording material for such an interrelation. The plan of interrelation is simple. As the study of the world as a whole, in the manner already sketched, progresses, the appropriate chapters are read, discussed, and reproduced, and the routes of the various discoverers and explorers traced. No further word seems to the writer necessary in regard to the interrelation.

Dresden, July 15, 1899.

CONTENTS.

PAGE

Beliefs as to the World Four Hundred Years Ago . 9

Marco Polo 16

Columbus 24

Vasco da Gama 40

John and Sebastian Cabot's Voyages 44

Amerigo Vespucci 48

Ponce de Leon 54

Balboa 56

Magellan 62

Hernando Cortes 68

Francisco Pizarro 78

Ferdinand de Soto 84

The Great River Amazon, and El Dorado . . . 92

Verrazzano 102

The Famous Voyage of Sir Francis Drake—1577 . . 108

Henry Hudson 114

DISCOVERERS AND EXPLORERS.

BELIEFS AS TO THE WORLD FOUR HUNDRED YEARS AGO.

FOUR hundred years ago most of the people who lived in Europe thought that the earth was flat. They knew only the land that was near them. They knew the continent of Europe, a small part of Asia, and a strip along the northern shore of Africa.

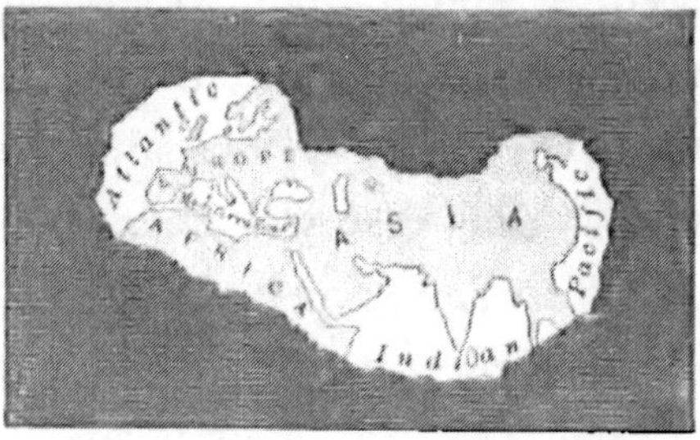

The World as Known Four Hundred Years ago.

They thought this known land was surrounded by a vast body of water that was like a broad river. Sailors were afraid to venture far upon this water, for they feared they would fall over the edge of the earth.

Other seafaring men believed that if they should sail too far out upon this water their vessels would be lost in a fog, or that they would suddenly begin to slide downhill, and would never be able to return.

Wind gods and storm gods, too, were supposed to dwell upon this mysterious sea. Men believed that these wind and storm gods would be very angry with any one who dared to enter their domain, and that in their wrath they would hurl the ships over the edge of the earth, or keep them wandering round and round in a circle, in the mist and fog.

It is no wonder that the name "Sea of Darkness" was given to this great body of water, which we now know to be the Atlantic Ocean; nor is it surprising that the sailors feared to venture far out upon it.

These sailors had no dread at all of a sea called the Mediterranean, upon which they made voyages without fear of danger. This sea was named the Mediterranean because it was supposed to be in the middle of the land that was then known. On this body of water the sailors were very bold, fighting, robbing, and plundering strangers and foes, without any thought of fear.

They sailed through this sea eastward to Constantinople, their ships being loaded with metals, woods, and pitch. These they traded for silks, cashmeres, dyewoods, spices, perfumes, precious stones, ivory, and pearls. All of these things were brought by caravan from the far Eastern countries, as India, China, and Japan, to the cities on the east coast of the Mediterranean.

This caravan journey was a very long and tiresome one. Worse than this, the Turks, through whose country the caravans passed, began to see how valuable this trade was, and they sent bands of robbers to prevent the caravans from reaching the coast.

A Caravan.

As time went on, these land journeys grew more difficult and more dangerous, until the traders saw that the day would soon come when they would be entirely cut off from traffic with India and the rich Eastern countries. The Turks would secure all their profitable business. So the men of that time tried to think of some other way of reaching the East.

Among those who wished to find a short route to India was Prince Henry of Portugal, a bold navigator as well as a studious and thoughtful man. He was desirous of securing the rich Indian trade for

Eric the Red in Vinland.

his own country. So he established a school for navigators at Lisbon, and gathered around him many men who wanted to study about the sea.

Here they made maps and charts, and talked with

one another about the strange lands which they thought might be found far out in that mysterious body of water which they so dreaded and feared. It is probable that they had heard some accounts of the voyages of other navigators on this wonderful sea, and the beliefs about land beyond.

There was Eric the Red, a bold navigator of Iceland, who had sailed west to Greenland, and planted there a colony that grew and thrived. There was also Eric's son Leif, a venturesome young viking who had made a voyage south from Greenland, and reached a strange country with wooded shores and fragrant vines. This country he called Vinland because of the abundance of wild grapes. When he returned to Greenland, he took a load of timber back with him.

Some of the people of Greenland had tried to make a settlement along this shore which Leif discovered, but it is thought that the Indians drove them away. It may now be said of this settlement that no trace of it has ever been found, although the report that the Norsemen paid many visits to the shore of North America is undoubtedly true.

Another bold sea rover of Portugal sailed four hundred miles from land, where he picked up a strangely carved paddle and several pieces of wood of a sort not to be found in Europe.

St. Brandon, an Irish priest, was driven in a storm far, far to the west, and landed upon the shore of a strange country, inhabited by a race of people different from any he had ever seen.

All this time the bold Portuguese sailors were venturing farther and farther down the coast of Africa. They hoped to be able to sail around that continent and up the other side to India. But they dared not go beyond the equator, because they did not know the stars in the southern hemisphere and therefore had no guide. They also believed that beyond the equator there was a frightful region of intense heat, where the sun scorched the earth and where the waters boiled.

Many marvelous stories were told about the islands which the sailors said they saw in the distance. Scarcely a vessel returned from a voyage without some new story of signs of land seen by the crew.

The people who lived on the Canary Islands said that an island with high mountains on it could be seen to the west on clear days, but no one ever found it.

Some thought these islands existed only in the imagination of the sailors. Others thought they were floating islands, as they were seen in many different places. Every one was anxious to find them, for they were said to be rich in gold and spices.

You can easily understand how excited many people were in regard to new lands, and how they wished to find out whether the earth was round or not. There was but one way to find out, and that was to try to sail around it.

For a long time no one was brave enough to venture to do so. To start out and sail away from land on this unknown water was to the people of that day as dangerous and foolhardy a journey as to try to cross the ocean in a balloon is to us at the present time.

MARCO POLO.

In the middle of the thirteenth century, about two hundred years before the time of Columbus, a boy named Marco Polo lived in the city of Venice.

Marco Polo belonged to a rich and noble family, and had all the advantages of study that the city afforded. He studied at one of the finest schools in the city of Venice. This city was then famous for its schools, and was the seat of culture and learning for the known world.

Marco Polo.

When Marco Polo started for school in the morning, he did not step out into a street, as you do. Instead, he stepped from his front doorstep into a boat called a gondola; for Venice is built upon a cluster of small islands, and the streets are water ways and are called canals.

The gondolier, as the man who rows the gondola

is called, took Marco wherever he wished to go. Sometimes, as they glided along, the gondolier would sing old Venetian songs; and as Marco Polo lay back against the soft cushions and listened and looked about him, he wondered if anywhere else on earth there was so beautiful a city as Venice. For the sky was very blue, and often its color

A Scene in Venice.

was reflected in the water; the buildings were graceful and beautiful, the sun was warm and bright, and the air was balmy.

In this delightful city Marco Polo lived until he was seventeen years of age. About this time, his father, who owned a large commercial house in Constantinople, told Marco that he might go with him on a long journey to Eastern countries. The boy was very glad to go, and set out with his father and his uncle, who were anxious to trade and gain more wealth in the East. This was in the year 1271.

The three Polos traveled across Persia into China, and across the Desert of Gobi to the northwest, where they found the great ruler, Kublai Khan. This monarch was a kind-hearted and able man. He wanted to help his subjects to become civilized and learned, as the Europeans were. So Kublai Khan assisted the two elder Polos in their business of trading, and took Marco into his service.

Soon Marco learned the languages of Asia, and then he was sent by the khan on errands of state to different parts of the country. He visited all the great cities in China, and traveled into the interior of Asia to places almost unknown at the present time.

At length the three Polos expressed a desire to return to Venice. The great khan did not wish to part with them, but he at last consented; for he found that by going they could do him a service. The service required was their escort for a beautiful young princess who was to be taken from Peking to Tabriz, where she was to marry the Khan of Persia.

It was difficult to find any one trustworthy enough to take charge of so important a person on so long and dangerous a journey. But Kublai Khan had faith in the Polos. They had traveled more than any one else he knew, and were cautious and brave.

So he gave them permission to return to their home, and requested them to take the princess to Tabriz on the way. It was decided that the journey should be made by sea, as the land route was so beset by robbers as to be unsafe. Besides, the Polos were fine sailors.

They started from the eastern coast of China, and continued their voyage for three years, around the peninsula of Cochin China, and through the Indian Ocean to the Persian Gulf. Here they went ashore, and then proceeded by land across Persia to Tabriz. They left the princess in that city, and resumed their journey by way of the Bosporus to Venice.

When they reached Venice they found that they had been forgotten by their friends. They had been away twenty-four years, and in that time everything had changed very much. They themselves had grown older, and their clothes differed from those worn by the Venetians; for fashions changed even in the thirteenth century, although not so often as they change at the present time. It is no wonder that the Polos were not known until they recalled themselves to the memory of their friends.

One evening they invited a few of their old friends

to dinner, and during the evening they brought out three old coats. These coats they proceeded to rip apart, and out from the linings dropped all kinds of precious stones—diamonds, sapphires, emeralds, and rubies. In this way these wary travelers had hidden their wealth and treasure while on their perilous journey. The visitors were astonished at the sight of so great riches, and listened eagerly to the accounts of the countries from which they came.

Soon after the return of Marco Polo to Venice, he took part with his countrymen in a battle against the Genoese. The city of Genoa, like the city of Venice, had a large trade with the East. These two cities were rivals in trade, and were very jealous of each other. Whenever Venetian ships and those of the Genoese met on the Mediterranean Sea, the sailors found some way of starting a quarrel. The quarrel quickly led to a sea fight, and it was in one of these combats that Marco Polo engaged. The Venetians were defeated, and Marco Polo was taken prisoner and cast into a dungeon. Here he spent his time in writing the wonderful book in which he described his travels.

The descriptions Polo gave of the East were as wonderful as fairy tales. He told of countries rich in gold, silver, and precious stones, and of islands where diamonds sparkled on the shore. The rulers

A Sea Fight.

of these countries wore garments of rich silk covered with glittering gems, and dwelt in palaces, the roofs of which were made of gold.

He described golden Cathay, with its vast cities rich in manufactures, and also Cipango, Hindustan, and Indo-China. He knew of the Indies Islands, rich in spices, and he described Siberia, and told of the sledges drawn by dogs, and of the polar bears. The fact that an ocean washed the eastern coast of Asia was proved by him, and this put at rest forever the theory that there was an impassable swamp east of Asia.

This book by Marco Polo was eagerly read, and the facts that it stated were so remarkable that many people refused to believe them. It stirred others with a desire to travel and see those lands for themselves.

Traveling by land, however, was very dangerous, because of the bands of robbers by which the country was occupied. These outlaws robbed every one whom they suspected of having any money, and often murdered travelers in order to gain their possessions. Sea travel, too, was just as dangerous, but in a different way.

You will remember why sailors dared not venture far out upon the ocean and search for a water route to the Eastern countries and islands. The time was soon coming, however, when they would dare to do so, and two wonderful inventions helped navigators very much.

One came from the finding of the loadstone, or natural magnet. This is a stone which has the power of attracting iron. A steel needle rubbed on it becomes magnetized, as we say, and, when suspended by the center and allowed to move freely, always swings around until it points north and south. Hung on a pivot and inclosed in a box, this instrument is called the mariners' compass. It was of great importance to sailors, because it always told them which way was north. On cloudy days, and during dark, stormy nights, when the sun and stars could not be seen, the sailors could now keep on their way, far from land, and still know in which direction they were going.

Mariners' Compass.

The other invention was that of the astrolabe. This was an instrument by means of which sailors measured the height of the sun above the horizon at noon, and could thus tell the distance of the ship from the equator. It is in use on all the ships at the present time, but it has been greatly improved, and is now called the quadrant.

The compass and the astrolabe, together with improved maps and charts, made it possible for navigators to tell where their ship was when out of sight of land or in the midst of storm and darkness. This made them more courageous, and they ventured a little farther from the coast, but still no one dared to sail far out upon the Sea of Darkness.

COLUMBUS.

Christopher Columbus.

ONE day a man appeared in Portugal, who said he was certain that the earth was round, and that he could reach India by sailing westward. Every one laughed at him and asked him how he would like to try. He answered that he would sail round the earth, if any one would provide him with ships.

People jeered and scoffed.

"If the earth is a sphere," they said, "in order to sail round it you must sail uphill! Who ever heard of a ship sailing uphill?"

But this man, whose name was Christopher Columbus, remained firm in his belief.

When a boy, Columbus had listened eagerly to the stories the sailors told about strange lands and wonderful islands beyond the water. He was in the habit of sitting on the wharves and watching the ships. Often he would say, "I wish, oh, how I wish I could be a sailor!"

At last his father, who was a wool comber, said to him, "My son, if you really wish to become a sailor, I will send you to a school where you will be taught navigation."

Columbus was delighted at this, and told his father that he would study diligently. He was sent to the University of Pavia, where he learned all the geography that was then known, as well as how to draw maps and charts. He became a skillful penman, and also studied astronomy, geometry, and Latin.

But he did not spend a long time at his studies, for at the age of fourteen he went to sea. What he had learned, however, gave him an excellent groundwork, and from this time forward he made use of every opportunity to inform himself and to become a scholarly man.

His first voyage was made with a distant relative, who was an adventurous and daring man, and who was ever ready to fight with any one with whom he could pick a quarrel. In course of time Columbus commanded a ship of his own, and became known as a bold and daring navigator. He made a voyage along the coast of Africa as far south as Guinea, and afterwards sailed northward to Iceland.

At an early day he became familiar with the wildest kind of adventure, for at this time sea life on the Mediterranean was little more than a series of fights with pirates. Some say that during one of these conflicts Columbus's ship caught fire. In order to save his life, he jumped into the water and swam six miles to shore, reaching the coast of Portugal. Others say that he was attracted to that country by the great school of navigation which Prince Henry had established. However that may be, he appeared at Lisbon at the age of thirty-five, filled with the idea of sailing westward to reach those rich Eastern countries in which every one was so much interested.

He was laughed at for expressing such an idea. It is not pleasant to be laughed at, but Columbus was courageous and never wavered in his belief.

"The earth is a sphere," he said; "those foolish stories of its being flat and supported on a turtle's back cannot be true."

But those persons to whom he talked only laughed the more.

"Is there anything more foolish," they asked, "than to believe that there are people who walk with their heels up and with their heads hanging down?" "Think of a place where the trees grow with their branches down, and where it snows, hails, and rains upward!"

Everybody thought him an idle dreamer.

Columbus tried to persuade King John to furnish him with ships and allow him to test his belief. But King John cruelly deceived Columbus; for, after obtaining his maps and charts, he sent off an expedition of his own. He hoped in this way to gain the glory of the discovery. The sailors whom he sent, however, were not brave enough to continue the voyage, and returned, frightened by a severe storm.

Columbus was so disgusted by the treachery of King John that he made up his mind to leave Portugal and go to Spain. So, taking his little son, Diego, with him, he started on his journey. He traveled from place to place, trying to find some person who would help him make his ideas known to King Ferdinand and Queen Isabella. He thought that if he could talk with them he could persuade them to furnish him with ships.

Convent of La Rábida.

One day he came to a convent called La Rábida.

Columbus before Ferdinand and Isabella.

Here Diego, who was weary and thirsty, begged his father to stop and ask for a drink of water. Columbus knocked at the big iron gate, and while he was conversing with the attendant a priest approached.

This priest was attracted by the noble bearing and refined speech of Columbus, and saw at once that he was not a beggar. He asked him what he wished, and Columbus related his story.

The good priest believed in him and said he would try to influence the king and queen to furnish him with ships. The priest brought the matter before the king; but at this time Spain was at war with the Moors, and King Ferdinand had no time to attend to anything else. Columbus was patient and waited. But as year after year passed and brought no prospect of obtaining the ships he wished, his hopes fell. After seven long, weary years of waiting, he was about to leave Spain in despair.

Just as he was leaving, however, a message was brought to him from the queen, asking him to explain his plans to her once more. Columbus did so, and the queen was so fully convinced that she exclaimed: "I will provide ships and men for you, if I have to pledge my jewels in order to do so!"

Three ships were fitted out for the voyage. These ships were very different from those we see to-day. They were light, frail barks called caravels, and two of them, the *Pinta* and *Niña*, had no decks. The third, the *Santa Maria*, had a deck. It was upon this largest caravel that Columbus placed his flag.

On the 3d of August, 1492, the little fleet set sail from Palos, entering upon the most daring expedition ever undertaken by man. The people of the town gathered on the wharf to see the departure of the vessels. Many of them had friends or relatives on board whom they expected never to look upon again. Sad indeed was the sight as the little caravels sailed out of the harbor and faded from view.

After sailing a few days, the *Pinta* broke her rudder. This accident the sailors took to be a sign of misfortune. They tried to persuade Columbus to put back to Palos, but he would not listen to such a suggestion. Instead of sailing back, he pushed on to the Canary Islands. Here his ships were delayed three weeks, after which they continued the voyage into unknown waters.

After they had sailed westward for many days, the sailors began to show signs of alarm, and they implored Columbus to return. He tried to calm their fears. He described the rich lands he hoped to find, and reminded them of the wealth and fame this voyage would bring to them. So they agreed to venture a little farther.

At last the compass began to point in a different

direction, and the sailors became almost panic-stricken. They thought they were sailing straight to destruction, and when they found that Columbus

The Pinta.

would not listen to their entreaties they planned a mutiny. Though Columbus knew what the sailors were plotting, he kept steadily on his course. Fortunately, signs of land soon began to appear. A branch with berries on it floated past, a rudely carved paddle was picked up, and land birds were seen flying over the ships.

A prize had been offered to the sailor who first saw land, and all eagerly watched for it night and day. At last, early one morning, a gun was fired from

The Landing of Columbus.

the *Pinta*, and all knew that land had been sighted. The sailors were filled with the wildest joy, and crowded around Columbus with expressions of gratitude and admiration, in great contrast to the distrustful manner in which they had treated him a few days before.

The land they were approaching was very beautiful. It was a green, sunny island with pleasant groves in which birds were singing. Beautiful flowers were blooming all around and the trees were laden with fruit. The island was inhabited, too, for groups of strange-looking men were seen running to the shore.

At length the ships cast anchor, the boats were lowered, and Columbus, clad in rich scarlet and carrying in his hand the royal banner of Spain, was taken ashore. As soon as he stepped on the beach, Columbus knelt down and gave thanks to God. He then planted the banner of Spain in the ground and took possession of the country in the name of Ferdinand and Isabella.

This island he called San Salvador, because he and his crew had been saved from a watery grave, and also because October 12 was so named in the Spanish calendar.

Columbus supposed San Salvador to be one of the islands near the coast of Asia, but it is one of the Bahamas.

Thus was America discovered on the 12th of October, 1492.

The natives of this island were different from any people the Spaniards had ever seen. They were of a reddish-brown color, and had high cheek bones, small black eyes, and straight black hair. They were entirely naked, and their bodies were greased and painted. Their hair was decorated with feathers, and many of them were adorned with curious ornaments.

They were at first very much afraid of the white men and kept far away. But gradually they lost their fear and brought the Spaniards presents of bananas and oranges. Some of them gathered courage enough to touch the Spaniards and pass their hands over them, as if to make certain that they were real beings. These men, whose skin was so white, they thought to be gods who had come down from the sky.

When Columbus asked them where they found the gold of which many of their ornaments were made, they pointed toward the south. Then Columbus took some of them with him to search for the land of gold.

The next land he reached was the island of Cuba. Thinking that this was a part of India, he called the natives Indians. He then sailed to Haiti, which he called Hispaniola, or "Little Spain." For more than three months Columbus cruised among these islands, where the air was always balmy, the sky clear, and the land beautiful. The sailors believed these new lands were Paradise, and wanted to live there always.

At length, however, they thought of returning to their home and friends. So, taking several Indians with them, and many curious baskets and ornaments, they set out on their return voyage.

This voyage proved to be very stormy, and at one time it seemed certain that the ships would go down; but after a time the sea grew quiet, and on the 15th of March they sailed again into the little harbor of Palos.

You can imagine the excitement.

"What! has Columbus returned?" asked the people. "Has he really found the East by sailing westward?"

"Yes, he has," was the answer. "He has found India."

Columbus was given a royal welcome. The king and queen held a great celebration in his honor at Barcelona; and when the Indians marched into court the astonishment of every person was great. The Indians were half naked; their dark bodies were painted, and their heads were adorned with feathers. They carried baskets of seed pearls, and wore strange ornaments of gold. Some carried the skins of wild animals, and others carried beautiful birds of brilliant plumage. Every inhabitant of Barcelona rejoiced, and the bells were rung in honor of the great discoverer.

It was a happy time for Columbus. He felt repaid for all his suffering and trouble.

King Ferdinand and Queen Isabella now wished Columbus to go again to these newly discovered islands and search for the gold that was thought to be there. You may be sure Columbus was willing to

The Return of Columbus.

go. So they fitted out seventeen vessels, manned by fifteen hundred men, and placed Columbus in command of this fleet. It was no trouble to find men who were willing to go on this voyage. All wanted to see the new world that had been found.

During this second voyage, which was made in 1493, Columbus discovered Jamaica, Puerto Rico, and some small islands in the Caribbean Sea.

On the island of Jamaica the Spaniards came upon the footprints of some strange animal which they thought to be a dragon. This dragon they believed was guarding the gold which they supposed was on the island. So they ran back to their ships in fear.

Later on they became used to seeing these footprints, and found that they were those of alligators. At Puerto Rico they suffered from a savage attack made by the natives, who shot poisoned arrows and threw javelins at them. But in most other places the natives were very friendly.

Columbus thought this land was a part of the east coast of Asia, and he could not understand why he did not find cities such as Marco Polo had described.

Columbus then sailed to Hispaniola, where he planted a colony, of which he was made governor. It was not an easy matter to govern this island, because of the jealousies and quarrels of the Spaniards.

At length Columbus returned to Spain, ill and discouraged.

Columbus made a third voyage in 1498, during which he sailed along the coast of Brazil, and discovered Trinidad Island. Here his ships encountered currents of fresh water which flowed with great force into the ocean. This led Columbus to think that so large a river must flow across a great conti-

Map Showing how Columbus Discovered America.

nent, and strengthened his opinion that the land was a part of the great continent of Asia.

After sailing farther north along the Pearl Coast, which was so called because of the pearls found there, he returned to Hispaniola. Here he found the Spaniards engaged in an Indian war, and quarreling among themselves. Some officials became jealous of him, bound him with chains, and sent him back to Spain a prisoner. Ferdinand and Isabella were much displeased at this treatment of Columbus, and set him free.

A fourth voyage was made by Columbus in 1502, during which he explored the coast of Honduras in search of a strait leading to the Indian Ocean. In this venture he was unsuccessful. On his return to Spain he found his friend Queen Isabella very ill, and nineteen days after his arrival she died.

After Isabella's death the king treated Columbus cruelly and ungratefully. The people had become jealous of him, and his last days were spent in poverty and distress. He never knew that he had discovered a new continent, but supposed that he had found India.

Seven years after his death the king repented of his ingratitude, and caused the remains of Columbus to be removed from the little monastery in Valladolid to a monastery in Seville, where a magnificent monument was erected to his memory. In 1536 his bones were removed to the Cathedral of San Domingo in Hispaniola, and later they were taken to the cathedral in Havana.

When the United States took possession of Cuba, the Spanish disinterred the bones of Columbus again and carried them to Spain, placing them in the cathedral of Seville, where they now are.

VASCO DA GAMA.

Vasco da Gama.

Both the Spaniards and the Portuguese were cut off from trade with the East, because the Turks had taken possession of Constantinople. In consequence of this, the navigators of both countries were making earnest efforts to find a water route to India.

Spain, as you know, had faith in Columbus, and helped him in his plan of trying to reach India by sailing westward. But the Portuguese had a different idea. They spent their time and money in trying to sail round the African coast, in the belief that India could be reached by means of a southeast passage.

This southeast passage could be found only by crossing the "burning zone," as the part of the earth near the equator was called; and all sailors feared to make the attempt.

It was thought almost impossible to cross this burning zone, and the few navigators who had ventured as far as the equator had turned back in fear of steaming whirlpools and of fiery belts of heat.

In 1486, six years before Columbus discovered America, the King of Portugal sent Bartholomew Diaz, a bold and daring navigator, to find the end of the African coast.

Bartholomew Diaz sailed through the fiery zone without meeting any of the dreadful misfortunes which the sailors so feared. When he had sailed beyond the tropic of Capricorn, a severe storm arose. The wind blew his three vessels directly south for thirteen days, during which time he lost sight of land. When the sun shone again, Diaz headed his vessels eastward, but as no land appeared, he again changed the direction, this time heading them toward the north. After sailing northward a short time, land was reached about two hundred miles east of the Cape of Good Hope.

Diaz now pushed on four hundred miles farther along the coast of Africa, and saw the wide expanse of the Indian Ocean before him. Here the sailors refused to go any farther, and Diaz, although he wanted very much to go ahead and try to reach India, was obliged to return.

On the way home, the vessels passed close to the

cape which projects from the south coast of Africa, and Diaz named it Stormy Cape, in memory of the frightful storm which hid it from view on the way down. When they reached Lisbon, however, King John said that it should be called the Cape of Good Hope, because they now had hope that the southern route to India was found.

Spanish and Portuguese Vessels.

Diaz won much praise for his bravery and patience in making this voyage. He had proved that the stories about the fiery zone were false, and that the African coast had an end.

It remained, however, for Vasco da Gama, then a young man of about twenty years of age, to prove that India could be reached in this way.

In 1497 Da Gama sailed from Lisbon to the Cape of Good Hope, doubled the cape, and proceeded across the Indian Ocean to Hindustan.

He returned to Lisbon in 1499, his ships loaded with the rich products of the East, including cloves, spices, pepper, ginger, and nutmeg. He also brought with him rich robes of silk and satin, costly gems, and many articles made of carved ivory, or of gold and of silver.

The King of Portugal was greatly pleased with what Da Gama had accomplished, and his successful voyage was the wonder of the day.

Costume of Explorers.

The same year that Da Gama returned from India by a route around the south end of Africa, with his ships loaded with rich produce, Sebastian Cabot returned from a fruitless voyage to the strange, barren coast of North America.

It was no wonder that the voyages of Columbus and the Cabots were thought unsuccessful as compared with the voyage Da Gama had just finished.

No one then dreamed of a New World; all were searching for the Orient—for golden Cathay.

JOHN AND SEBASTIAN CABOT'S VOYAGES.

JOHN CABOT was a Venetian merchant, and a bold seafaring man. For purposes of trade he had taken up his home in Bristol, England. Bristol at that time was the most important seaport of England, and carried on a large fishing trade with Iceland.

Sebastian Cabot.

When the news of the voyage of Columbus reached Bristol, Cabot begged the English king, Henry VII., to let him go and see if he could find a shorter route to the Indies. The king gave his consent, and told Cabot to take possession of any land he might discover for England.

Cabot fitted out his vessel and, taking his son Sebastian and a crew of eighteen men with him, set sail in 1497. He headed his ship westward, hoping to reach the Spice Islands and that part of Asia which was so rich in gold, and which Columbus had failed to find. At last, one sunny morning in June, land was sighted in the distance.

This land, which was probably a part of Nova Scotia, proved to be a lonely shore with dense forests. Cabot called it "Land First Seen." It was entirely deserted, not a human being nor a hut of any kind being in sight.

Here Cabot and his son Sebastian and some of his crew went ashore, and were the first white men, excepting the Norsemen, to step upon the mainland of America. Up to this time, Columbus had discovered only islands of the West Indies. A year later than this he discovered the continent of South America. Cabot and his companions erected a large cross on the shore, and planted two flagpoles in the ground, from which they unfurled the English and Venetian flags. Then they returned to their ships, and, after sailing about the Gulf of St. Lawrence, went back to England.

King Henry and the people received John Cabot with great honor. Everybody thought that Cabot had reached Asia, and he also believed that he had. He was called the "Great Admiral," and the people of Bristol ran after him on the street, shouting his name and trying in every way to show him how much they admired and honored him. The king gave him fifty dollars in money, which seems to us in these days a small sum for so long and dangerous a voyage. Besides this, the king urged him to undertake another voyage.

About a year later Sebastian Cabot made the second voyage, and this time the gloomy shore of Labrador was reached.

Sebastian on his voyage sailed far north, passing many icebergs, and seeing many strange and wonderful sights.

On great blocks of ice that floated past the ship he saw immense white bears. These bears were fine swimmers, and would often leap into the water and bring out fish, which they would devour greedily. The waters were filled with fish, and, as the ship neared the shore, they grew so numerous as almost to retard the sailing of the vessel.

"Now," said Cabot, "the English will not have to go to Iceland any more for fish."

But Cabot knew that the lands he was seeking were warm lands. So he turned his vessel south, hoping to reach some opening which would lead to them. To his great surprise, he found the coast very long and without any opening, and he sailed on and on as far as Maryland, taking possession of the land for England.

At places along this shore were seen Indians, clad

in skins and furs of wild animals, fishing from little canoes. Stags much larger than any in England were seen in great numbers, and wild turkeys and game of all sorts abounded.

Then Sebastian Cabot began to think that this was a part of Asia never known before, and he set sail for home to tell the wonderful news.

When he reached Bristol he found everybody still interested in India. It was a water route to India that was wanted, and not a new country. People cared more about reaching golden Cathay than about finding new, barren lands.

So, although King Henry was proud to know that the new land belonged to England, it was eleven years before he made any further attempt to send ships there to take possession.

AMERIGO VESPUCCI.

AMERIGO VESPUCCI was a native of Florence, Italy, and a friend of Columbus. He was an educated man and very fond of study.

At the time in which he lived it was difficult to find the latitude and longitude of places, and few people were able to calculate either correctly. Vespucci was skillful in the work of computing longitude, and he was also well versed in the history of all the voyages that had been made. He was familiar with the facts of astronomy and geography then known, and was well able to conduct the sailing of a ship into strange waters.

Amerigo Vespucci.

It is believed that Vespucci made six voyages. He did not command his own vessels, as Columbus did, but he went with the expedition as assistant or adviser to the captain, keeping records of the voyage and making maps and charts.

In his first voyage, made in 1497, Vespucci reached the coast of Honduras, and sailed into the Gulf of Mexico. Here he found, probably on the coast of Yucatan, a queer little sea village which reminded him of the great city of Venice near his home.

A Queer Little Sea Village.

The houses in this village were made of wood, and were built on piles running out into the water. These houses were connected with the shore by bridges, which were constructed in such a manner that they could be drawn up, thus cutting off all connection with the land. In one house Vespucci found six hundred people. A very large family, was it not?

Continuing the voyage around the Gulf of Mexico, many strange and wonderful sights were seen. The natives roasted and ate frightful animals, which from the description given us we now know to have been alligators. They also made cakes, or patties, out of fish, and baked them on red-hot coals. The Spaniards were invited to taste these dainties, and those of the sailors who did so found the strange food very palatable.

After sailing round the coast of Florida, the ships headed northeast, landing every now and then for the purpose of trading with the Indians. The Spaniards, finding but little gold and none of the rich spices for which they were looking, at last decided to return home.

Just before sailing, some friendly Indians helped the Spaniards to make an attack upon a cannibal island. The attack was successful, and about two hundred cannibals were taken prisoners and carried to Spain, where they were sold as slaves.

Vespucci made a second voyage in 1499, in which he sailed down the African coast to the Cape Verde Islands, and then headed his ship almost directly west. He sighted land at Cape St. Roque, and then sailed northwest, exploring the north coast of South America, then called the Pearl Coast. After this he returned to Spain.

Shortly after the return of Vespucci to Spain, he accepted an offer to take service under the Portuguese flag.

In 1501 he set sail from Lisbon with three caravels, under this flag. He reached the coast of South America near Cape St. Roque, and sailed south as far as the South Georgia Islands.

As he proceeded southward, he found the country was inhabited by fierce Indians, who ate their fellow-creatures. He did not like the natives, as you may suppose; but he thought the country was beautiful, with the wonderful verdure and foliage of the tropics, and the queer animals and bright-colored birds.

Great was the joy of Vespucci when he discovered in the forests large quantities of a sort of red dye-wood which was prized very highly by Europeans. This wood, which had hitherto been found only in Eastern countries, was called brazil wood; and because of its abundance there, he gave the name Brazil to that part of the country.

The expedition sailed slowly on and at length lost sight of land. It is thought that Vespucci headed the ships southeast because he wished to find out whether there was land or not in the Antarctic Ocean.

As they sailed farther and farther south, the climate became very disagreeable. The winds grew cold and forbidding, fields of floating ice hindered the progress of the vessel, and the nights became very long.

The sailors grew frightened, fearing that they were entering a land of constant darkness. Their fear became greater when a terrific storm arose. The sea grew rough, and the fog and sleet prevented the sailors from seeing whether land was near or not. The land which they had hoped to find now became an added danger.

One day, through the sleet and snow, the sailors saw with terror a rocky, jagged coast in front of them.

This land proved to be the South Georgia Islands, and was a wretched and forlorn country composed of rocks and glaciers, and entirely deserted. For a day and a half they sailed in sight of this frightful shore, fearing each moment that their ship would be cast on the rocks and that they would all perish. As soon as the weather permitted, therefore, Vespucci signaled his fleet, and the ships were headed for home, reaching Portugal in 1502.

This voyage secured Brazil for Portugal, and added greatly to the geographical knowledge of the day.

The ancients had said that no continent existed south of the equator. But the great length of coast along which Vespucci had sailed proved that the land was not an island. It was plainly a continent, and south of the equator.

Vespucci called the land he found the New World. For a time it was also called the Fourth Part of the Earth, the other three parts being Europe, Asia, and Africa. In 1507 a German writer published an account of the discovery, in which he called the new country America, in honor of Americus Vespucius,[1] the discoverer.

This land was not connected in any way with the discovery of Columbus, for he was supposed to have found Asia.

The name America was at first applied only to that part of the country which we now call Brazil, but little by little the name was extended until it included the whole of the Western Continent.

You will be glad to know that Vespucci, in the time of his success, did not forget his old friend Columbus, who was then poor and in disgrace. Vespucci visited him and did all he could to assist him.

After Vespucci had made three other voyages to the New World, he was given an important government position in Spain, which he held during the remainder of his life.

[1] Americus Vespucius is the Latin form of Amerigo Vespucci.

PONCE DE LEON.

You have heard many surprising things which the people of the fifteenth century believed. It seems almost impossible for us to think that those people really had faith in a Fountain of Youth; yet such is the case.

Ponce de Leon.

This fountain was supposed to exist somewhere in the New World, and it was thought that if any one should bathe in its waters, he would become young and would never grow old again.

In 1513 Ponce de Leon, who was then governor of Puerto Rico, sailed from that island in search of this Fountain of Youth. De Leon was an old man, and he felt that his life was nearly over, unless he should succeed in finding this fountain. At the same time De Leon wished to gain gold, for, though he had already made a fortune in Puerto Rico, he was still very greedy.

The expedition under his guidance sailed among the Bahamas and other islands near them, and at length reached a land beautiful with flowers, balmy with warm breezes, and cheerful with the song of birds. Partly because this discovery was made on Easter Sunday, which the Spaniards called Pascua Florida, and partly because of the abundance of flowers, De Leon called the land Florida.

He took possession of this delightful country for Spain, and then spent many weeks exploring its coast. After sailing north as far as St. Augustine, and finding neither gold nor the fabled Fountain of Youth, De Leon turned his vessels and proceeded south, doubling the Florida Cape. Shortly afterwards he became discouraged and returned to Puerto Rico.

In 1521 De Leon went again to Florida, this time for the purpose of planting a colony. The Indians were very angry that the white men should try to take their land, and they made a fierce attack upon De Leon and his party. In this attack De Leon received a severe wound, which compelled him to go to Cuba for care and rest. There he died after much suffering.

De Leon never found the Fountain of Youth, nor were the fabled waters discovered afterwards.

BALBOA.

The Spanish colonists on the island of Hispaniola made frequent visits to the mainland, searching for the rich cities of which Marco Polo had written.

Word reached the colonists that some of these gold hunters were starving at a place called Darien, and a ship was immediately sent to their relief. The cargo of the ship consisted of barrels of provisions and ammunition.

Imagine, if you can, the amazement of the commander of the expedition when, after his ships were under sail, a young and handsome man stepped out of one of the barrels. The young man was Vasco Nuñez Balboa. He had chosen this way to escape from Cuba, where he owed large sums of money which he could not pay. The commander was angry, and threatened to leave Balboa on a desert island; but at length he took pity on the young man, and allowed him to remain on board the ship.

When the mainland was reached, the Spaniards who were already there, having heard of the cruelty

Balboa Crossing the Isthmus.

of the commander, refused to let him land. He therefore put off to sea, and was never heard of again. Balboa then took command of the men and began immediately to explore the country.

He made a friendly alliance with an Indian chief, who presented him with gold and slaves. The Spaniards were delighted at the sight of so much riches. They began to melt and weigh the gold, and at last fell to quarreling desperately about the division of it.

This the Indians could not understand. They knew nothing of money, and valued the metal only because it could be made into beautiful ornaments.

An Indian boy who had heard the dispute told the Spaniards that if they cared so much about that yellow stuff, it would be wise for them to go to a country where there was enough of it for all.

The Spaniards eagerly questioned him regarding this place. The boy then described a country across the mountains and to the south, on the shores of a great sea, where the metal was so plentiful that the natives used it for their ordinary drinking cups and bowls.

Balboa immediately started southward across the mountains in search of this rich country. On his way he came upon a tribe of hostile Indians, who attacked him, but who fled in alarm from the guns of the Spaniards.

Taking some Indians as guides, Balboa pushed on through the mountains, and on September 25, 1513, from one of the highest peaks, looked down upon the Pacific Ocean.

Balboa Discovering the Pacific.

With his Spaniards he descended the mountain, and in four days reached the shore of that magnificent body of water. Balboa waded out into it with his sword in his hand, and formally took possession of it for the King of Spain. He called it the

South Sea, because he was looking toward the south when he first saw it; and the Pacific Ocean was known by this name for many years afterward.

On this shore he met an Indian who repeated to him the same story that the Indian boy had told about the rich country on the border of this sea and farther to the south.

Balboa then made up his mind to find this country. Accordingly he returned to Darien, and sent word to the Spanish king of his great discovery of the South Sea.

He then began to take his ships apart, and to send them, piece by piece, across the mountains to the Pacific coast.

This was an enormous undertaking. The journey was a very difficult one, and hundreds of the poor Indians who carried the burdens dropped dead from exhaustion.

At length, after long months of labor, four ships were thus carried across the mountains and rebuilt on the Pacific coast. These were the first European vessels ever launched on the great South Sea. Three hundred men were in readiness to go with Balboa on his voyage in search of the rich country of the South.

A little iron and a little pitch were still needed for the ships, and Balboa delayed his departure in order to get these articles.

The delay gave his enemies, who were jealous because of his success, time to carry out a plot against him. They accused him of plotting to set up an independent government of his own, and caused him to be arrested for treason. In less than twenty-four hours this brave and high-spirited leader was tried, found guilty, and beheaded. So ended all his ambitious plans.

MAGELLAN.

One of the boldest and most determined of all the early explorers was Ferdinand Magellan, a young Portuguese nobleman. He felt sure that somewhere on that long coast which so many explorers had reached he would find a strait through which he would be able to pass, and which would lead into the Indian Ocean; and so Magellan formed the idea of circumnavigating the globe.

Ferdinand Magellan.

He applied to the King of Portugal for aid; but as the Portuguese king was not willing to help him, he went to Spain, where his plan found favor.

The Spanish king gave him a fleet of five vessels, and on September 20, 1519, he set sail for the Canary Islands. Continuing the voyage toward Sierra Leone, the vessels were becalmed, and for a period of three weeks they advanced only nine miles. Then a terrific storm arose, and the sailors, who had grumbled and found fault with everything during the entire voyage, broke into open mutiny. This mutiny Magellan quickly quelled by causing the principal offender to be arrested and put in irons.

The voyage was then continued, and land was at last sighted on the Brazilian coast, near Pernambuco.

The fleet then proceeded down the coast as far as Patagonia, where the weather grew so very cold that it was decided to seek winter quarters and postpone the remainder of the journey until spring. This was done, Magellan finding a sheltered spot at Port St. Julian, where plenty of fish could be obtained and where the natives were friendly.

These native Patagonians Magellan described as being very tall, like giants, with long, flowing hair, and dressed scantily in skins.

Great hardships had been endured by the crew. Food and water had been scarce, the storms had been severe, and suffering from cold was intense. The sailors did not believe there was any strait, and they begged Magellan to sail for home. It was useless to try to influence this determined man. Danger made him only the more firm. Magellan told them that he would not return until he had found the opening for which he was looking.

Then the mutiny broke out anew. But Magellan

by his prompt and decisive action put it down in twenty-four hours. One offender was killed, and two others were put in irons and left to their fate on the shore when the ships sailed away.

As soon as the weather grew warmer the ships started again southward. After nearly two months of sailing, most of the time through violent storms, a narrow channel was found, in which the water was salt. This the sailors knew must be the entrance to a strait.

Food was scarce, and the men again begged Magellan to return; but he firmly refused, saying: "I will go on, if I have to eat the leather off the ship's yards."

So the ships entered and sailed through the winding passage, which sometimes broadened out into a bay and then became narrow again. Among the twists and windings of this perilous strait, one of the vessels, being in charge of a mutinous commander, escaped and turned back.

On both sides of the shore there were high mountains, the tops of which were covered with snow, and which cast gloomy shadows upon the water below them.

Think of the feelings of the crew when, after sailing five weeks through this winding channel, they came out into a calm expanse of water. Magellan was overcome by the sight, and shed tears of joy. He named the vast waters before him Pacific, which means "peaceful," because of their contrast to the violent and stormy Atlantic.

Strait of Magellan.

The fleet now sailed northwest into a warmer climate and over a tranquil ocean, and as week after week passed and no land was seen, the sailors lost all hope. They began to think that this ocean had no end, and that they might sail on and on forever.

These poor men suffered very much from lack of food and water, and many died of famine. The boastful remark of Magellan was recalled when the sailors did really begin to eat the leather from the ship's yards, first soaking it in the water.

Anxiously these worn and haggard men looked about for signs of land, and at length they were rewarded. The Ladrone Islands were reached, and supplies of fresh vegetables, meats, and fruits were obtained. From the Isles de Ladrones, or "Isles of Robbers," the fleet proceeded to the Philippines.

Here Magellan knew that he was near the Indian Ocean, and realized that if he kept on in his course he would circumnavigate the globe.

It was on one of the Philippine Islands that this "Prince of Navigators" lost his life in a skirmish with the natives. He was, as usual, in the thickest of the fight, and while trying to shield one of his men was struck down by the spear of a native.

One of his ships, the *Victoria*, continued the voyage around Cape of Good Hope, and on September 6, 1522, with eighteen weary and half-starved men on board, succeeded in reaching Spain.

Great hardships had been endured, but the wonderful news they brought made up in some measure for their suffering.

This was the greatest voyage since the first voyage of Columbus, and the strait still bears the name of the remarkable man whose courage and strength of purpose led to the accomplishment of one of the greatest undertakings ever recorded in history.

This wonderful voyage of Magellan's proved beyond doubt that the earth is round. It also proved that South America is a continent, and that there is no short southwest passage.

After this voyage all the navigators turned their attention to the discovery of a northwest passage.

HERNANDO CORTES.

THE Spaniards who lived on the island of Hispaniola sent frequent expeditions to the mainland in the hope of finding gold.

Hernando Cortes, a dashing young Spaniard with a love of adventure and a reckless daring seldom seen, was given command of one of these expeditions.

Hernando Cortes.

In March, 1519, he landed on the coast of Central America, with about six hundred men, ten heavy guns, and sixteen horses. Here Cortes found the natives in large numbers arrayed against him. A fierce battle was fought. But the firearms of the Spaniards frightened the barbarians, and when the cavalry arrived the Indians fled in terror. The Indians, who had never seen horses before, thought the man riding the horse was a part of the animal, and that these strange creatures were sent by the gods. Fear made the Indians helpless, and it was easy for Cortes to gain a victory over them.

After this victory Cortes sailed northward along the coast of San Juan de Ulloa. The natives of that region had heard of the wonderful white-skinned and bearded men who bore charmed lives, and they thought that these men were gods. They, therefore, treated the Spaniards in a friendly manner, and brought gifts of flowers, fruits, and vegetables, and also ornaments of gold and silver to Cortes.

Here Cortes landed and founded the city of Vera Cruz, which is to-day an important seaport of Mexico. The native Indians in this place were called Aztecs. Some of their chiefs, who paid a visit to Cortes, told him of the great Emperor Montezuma, who was rich and powerful, and who lived inland, in a wonderful city built in a lake.

By these chiefs Cortes sent to Montezuma presents of collars, bracelets, and ornaments of glass, an armchair richly carved, and an embroidered crimson cap. In return, Montezuma sent shields, helmets, and plates of pure gold, sandals, fans, gold ornaments of exquisite workmanship, together with robes of fine cotton interwoven with feather work, so skillfully done that it resembled painting. The cap which Cortes had sent was returned filled with gold dust.

The great Montezuma also sent a message to Cortes, saying that he would be glad to meet so brave a general, but that the road to the Mexican capital was too dangerous for an army to pass over. He also promised to pay a yearly tribute to the

Aztecs.

Spanish king if Cortes and his followers would depart and leave him in peace.

The Spaniards were jubilant when they saw the superb gifts. They felt certain that this great emperor must have enormous wealth at his command, and in spite of the warning message, most of them wished to start immediately for the Mexican capital. Some, however, thought such a course very unwise; Montezuma, they said, was so powerful a ruler that it was absurd to attack him with their small force, and they advised returning to Cuba for a large number of soldiers.

But Cortes had his own ideas on the subject. So he secretly ordered his ships to be sunk, and then, all chance of retreat being cut off, the entire force proceeded toward Mexico, August 16, 1519.

After a long march, the Spaniards began to ascend the plateau on which the city of Mexico is situated, and finally reached the top of it, seven thousand feet high.

They found the climate on this plateau temperate and balmy. The fields were cultivated, and beautiful flowers grew wild in profusion.

During the march the Spaniards passed many towns containing queer houses and temples. They entered many of the temples, threw down the idols, and took possession of ornaments of value. At length they saw in the distance a city which was built in a salt lake. Three avenues, built of stone, led across the water to it.

These avenues, which were four or five miles in length, were guarded on both sides by Indians in canoes. The avenues continued through the city, meeting in the center, where the great temple was situated.

The temple was inclosed by a huge stone wall, and contained twenty pyramids, each a hundred feet in height. Nearly all of the houses were two stories high, and were built of red stone. The roofs were flat, with towers at the corners, and on top of the roofs there were beautiful flower gardens.

Meeting of Cortes and Montezuma.

Into this remarkable town Cortes and his followers marched. Montezuma received his unwelcome guests with every mark of friendship, and with much pomp and ceremony. The great emperor was carried on a litter, which was richly decorated with gold and silver. The nobles of his court surrounded him, and hundreds of his retainers were drawn up in line behind him.

The first thing, when Cortes and Montezuma met, was the customary exchange of presents. Cortes presented Montezuma with a chain of colored glass beads, and in return the Aztec ruler gave Cortes a house which was large enough to accommodate all of the Spaniards.

For ten days these two men met each other and exchanged civilities, Cortes pretending to be paying a friendly visit, and Montezuma feeling puzzled and uncertain.

At length Cortes induced Montezuma to go to the house where the Spaniards were living, and then, when he got him there, refused to allow him to leave, thus keeping him a prisoner in his own city.

This daring act aroused the suspicions of the Aztecs. But Cortes used all his cunning to deceive these simple-hearted people and to make them continue to think that the Spaniards were gods. Still, the Aztecs were beginning to feel very bitter toward Cortes and his followers because of the disrespect with which they treated the Aztec temples and gods. The Spaniards were constantly throwing these gods out of the temples. Even their great god of war was not safe.

Cortes openly derided this image, calling it trash,

and proposing to erect the emblems of the Spanish religion in its place in the Aztec temples.

Now, the Aztec god of war was a frightful image with golden serpents entwined about the body. The face was hideous, and in its hand was carried a plate upon which were placed human hearts as sacrifices. But to the Aztecs the image was sacred, and this insult, together with many others which had been offered their gods, made the natives very angry.

One day the Aztecs discovered that some of the Spaniards had died. This knowledge dispelled the fear that their unbidden visitors were gods, and they attacked the Spaniards with great fury.

The Aztec warriors wore quilted cotton doublets and headdresses adorned with feathers. They carried leather shields, and fought fiercely with bows and arrows, copper-pointed lances, javelins, and slings. Though by comparison few in numbers, the Spaniards, who were protected by coats of mail, made great havoc with their guns and horses.

The battle between these unequal forces raged with great fury, and for a time the result was uncertain. Cortes compelled Montezuma, his prisoner, to show himself on the roof of his house and try to persuade the Aztecs to stop fighting.

The Indians, however, no longer feared their emperor, and instead of obeying him, they made him a target for their arrows and stones. In the midst of the fight, the great Montezuma was finally knocked down and killed by one of his former subjects.

Aztec Ruins.

After a desperate struggle, the Spaniards were forced to retreat. While making their escape over the bridges of the city they were attacked by Indian warriors in canoes, and more than half of their number were killed.

Notwithstanding this defeat and the loss of so many men, Cortes did not give up his design of conquering Mexico. He made an alliance with hostile tribes of Indians, and again attacked the city.

The Aztecs had now a new king, named Gua-te-mot-zin, who was as brave and determined as Cortes himself. Guatemotzin made preparations to oppose Cortes, and during the terrible siege which followed never once thought of surrendering or of asking for peace.

The Spaniards made attack after attack, and terrible battles were fought, in which the loss on both sides was very great. During one of these battles Cortes was nearly captured, and it seemed as though the war god was to be avenged upon the man who had so insulted him. But a young Spaniard rushed to the assistance of Cortes, and with one blow of his sword cut off the arms of the Indian who had dared to seize the Spanish leader.

After a time the Aztecs found themselves prisoners within their own city. The Spaniards had cut off all means of escape, and the Indians were starving to death. Their sufferings were terrible, and hundreds dropped down daily in the streets. Yet the proud king Guatemotzin refused to submit, and Cortes ordered a final attack. After furious fighting Guatemotzin was captured, and the Aztecs surrendered. Their cruel religion, with its strange gods and human sacrifices, was now overthrown.

Cortes, with his few followers, never more than one thousand trained soldiers, had succeeded in conquering a country larger than Spain. Over a million Mexicans had perished, and those that remained left the city and fled to the mountains.

In this way the magnificent civilization of the ancient Mexicans was destroyed. Shiploads of treasures were sent by Cortes to the Spanish king, Charles V., who rejoiced at the glory gained for his country.

FRANCISCO PIZARRO.

AMONG the men who had been with Balboa, and who had heard of the wonderful country of the Incas, was Francisco Pizarro. He determined to find this rich country and to conquer it.

Securing a band of about two hundred men, well armed and mounted on strong horses, he led them, in spite of terrible hardships, over mountains, through valleys, and across plateaus to Cajamarca, the city where the Inca, or king, was then staying.

Francisco Pizarro.

The natives gazed at the Spaniards in wonder and dread. These simple people thought that the white-faced, bearded strangers, who carried thunderbolts in their hands, and who rode such frightful-looking animals, were gods. In spite of their fear, the Indians received the strangers kindly, and gave them food and shelter.

That evening, Pizarro and De Soto, taking with them thirty-five horsemen, visited the Inca and arranged with him for a meeting next day in the open square. It was a strange visit. The Inca was surrounded by his slaves and chieftains, and was very polite to the strangers.

But the Spaniards began to feel very uneasy. An army composed of thousands of Indians was encamped only two miles away; and compared with it, the two hundred men of Pizarro appeared powerless. The situation of the Spaniards, should the Inca decide to oppose them, seemed without hope.

Pizarro scarcely slept that night. He lay awake planning how he might take the Inca prisoner.

The next day, about noon, the Indian procession approached the market place. First came attendants who cleared the way; then followed nobles and men of high rank, richly dressed, and covered with ornaments of gold and gems. Last came the Inca, carried on a throne of solid gold, which was gorgeously trimmed with the plumes of tropical birds.

The Indian monarch wore rich garments adorned with gold ornaments, and around his neck was a collar of superb emeralds of great size and brilliancy. He took his position near the center of the square, his escort, numbering several thousand, gathered around him.

Looking about, the Inca failed to see any of the Spaniards.

"Where are the strangers?" he asked.

Just then Pizarro's chaplain, with his Bible in his hand, approached the Inca. The chaplain said that he and his people had been sent by a mighty prince to beg the Inca to accept the true religion and consent to be tributary to the great emperor, Charles V., who would then protect them.

The Inca grew very angry at this, and declared that he would not change his faith nor be any man's tributary. He then indignantly threw the sacred book upon the ground, and demanded satisfaction from the Spaniards for this insult to him.

At this the priest gave the signal, and the Spaniards rushed from their hiding-places and attacked the panic-stricken Indians. The Inca and his attendants were wholly unprepared, being unarmed and utterly defenseless.

The Spaniards charged through them, showing no mercy, their swords slashing right and left, and their prancing horses trampling the natives under foot. The guns and firearms of the Spaniards made such havoc and confusion that the terrified Indians offered no resistance. Indeed, they could not offer any.

In the vicinity of the Inca the struggle was fierce. The Indians, faithful to the last to their beloved monarch, threw themselves before him, shielding him with their naked bodies from the swords of the Spaniards. At last, as night drew near, the Spaniards, fearing that the Inca might escape, attempted to kill him.

But Pizarro desired that he should be taken alive, and in a loud voice ordered his followers, as they

The Spaniards Attacking the Inca's Escort.

valued their own lives, not to strike the Inca. Stretching out his arm to save the monarch, Pizarro received a wound on his hand. This was the only wound received by a Spaniard during the attack.

At length the Inca was cast from his throne, and, falling to the ground, was caught by Pizarro. He was then imprisoned and placed under a strong guard. As soon as the news of the capture of the Inca spread, all resistance ceased. Many of the Indians fled to the mountains, leaving untold wealth at the disposal of their conquerors, while others remained, hoping to be able to assist their fallen ruler.

As soon as the Inca had an opportunity, he tried to think of some way of obtaining his freedom.

The room in which he was confined was twenty-two feet in length by seventeen feet in width. Raising his hand as high as he could, the Inca made a mark upon the wall, and told Pizarro that gold enough to fill the room to that mark would be given as a ransom for his release.

Pizarro agreed to this bargain, and the natives began to send gold to the Inca to secure his release. Some of the treasures in the temples were buried and hidden by the priests; but ornaments of all kinds, vases, and plate were collected, and in a few months gold amounting to fifteen millions of dollars in our money was divided among the Spaniards.

Millions of dollars' worth of gold and silver were shipped to Spain, and the Spanish nation grew very wealthy. Pizarro himself returned to Spain to take Charles V. his share of the plunder. During Pizarro's absence the Spaniards caused the Inca to be killed, notwithstanding the large ransom which they had accepted.

The richer the Spanish people grew, the more careless they became in their treatment of other nations and of those under their rule. They grew more cruel and more merciless and more greedy for gold. They flocked in great numbers to South America, a reckless, adventurous, unprincipled horde, ready to commit any crime in order to secure gold.

FERDINAND DE SOTO.

AMONG the men who had been with Pizarro in Peru was Ferdinand de Soto, a bold and dashing Spanish cavalier.

De Soto was appointed governor of Cuba in 1537, and at the same time received permission from the Spanish king to conquer Florida. This permission to conquer Florida was received by De Soto with great delight. He felt certain that in the interior of Florida there were cities as large and as wealthy as those of Peru. To conquer these cities, obtain their treasure, and win for himself riches and fame, was the dream of De Soto.

Ferdinand de Soto.

Strange as it may seem to you, De Soto was also anxious to convert the natives to his own religion. He intended to take from them all their possessions, but he meant to save their souls, if possible.

So, leaving his young and beautiful wife Isabella

to rule over Cuba in his absence, De Soto, in May, 1539, started from Havana with nine vessels, about six hundred men, and two hundred and twenty-three horses.

After a safe voyage, the expedition landed on the coast of Florida, at Tampa Bay. Before starting on the march to the interior of the country, De Soto sent all the vessels back to Cuba. In this way he cut off all hope of retreat, in case the men should become discouraged. But no one thought of wanting to return now. Everybody was in high spirits.

The soldiers wore brilliant uniforms, their caps were adorned with waving plumes, and their polished armor glistened and sparkled in the sunshine.

In the company were twelve priests, who were expected to convert the prisoners which De Soto meant to capture. The Spaniards carried with them chains to secure these prisoners, and bloodhounds to track them in case any escaped.

It was a gay company which marched off into the interior of Florida with prancing horses, waving flags and banners, and beating drums.

At first De Soto marched directly north, plunging into a wilderness which proved to be almost impassable. The country was full of swamps, through which the horses could scarcely travel. The large trees were bound together by tangled vines; and their roots, which protruded from the earth, were like traps, catching the feet of the travelers and throwing them to the ground.

Besides all this, the heavy baggage which the men and horses carried weighed them down and made the journey almost impossible.

De Soto, however, kept bravely on, encouraging his men as best he could, and at last reached the Savannah River. Here he changed his course to westward, hoping to find gold in that direction.

Week after week, month after month, the Spaniards traveled on through a dense wilderness, enduring great hardships and finding nothing but tribes of hostile Indians.

De Soto asked one of these Indian chiefs to give him slaves enough to carry his baggage through the forest. The chief refused; whereupon De Soto and his men attacked the tribe and took many prisoners. These prisoners De Soto caused to be chained together and placed in front of the expedition, where they were made to act as guides as well as slaves.

Then De Soto asked the Indians where the great cities with gold and silver treasures were. One Indian said he did not know of any. At this reply De Soto caused the Indian to be put to death with frightful torture. This made the Indians untruthful, and they told De Soto many different stories of places where they thought gold might be found.

So the expedition wandered on, searching for the gold which they never found; and the men grew discouraged and heartsick, and longed for home.

The Indian tribes, angry at the cruel treatment of the Spaniards, attacked them frequently, and De Soto and his men scarcely ever enjoyed a peaceful rest at

De Soto Marching through the Forest.

night. The Spaniards were unused to Indian warfare, and were no match for the quick, nimble savages, who glided through the forests silently and swiftly. These Indians never came to open battle, but hid themselves behind rocks and trees, and were

De Soto Discovers the Mississippi River.

scarcely ever seen. Two or three would suddenly appear, send a shower of arrows at the Spaniards, and then dart away again into the woods. The Indians scarcely ever missed their aim, and the Spaniards never knew when they were near.

One day De Soto captured some Indians who said that they knew where gold was to be found and that they would show the way to the place. De Soto only half trusted them, but he allowed them to lead the way. The cunning savages led the Spaniards into an ambush, where other Indians attacked them fiercely, killing their horses and many of their men.

As punishment for this act, De Soto ordered that these Indians should be torn to pieces by the bloodhounds.

Sometimes the Spaniards, in their wanderings, passed camps where the Indians were gathered round huge bonfires, singing, dancing, yelling, and shouting the terrible Indian war whoop. Under shelter of this noise the Spaniards would steal quietly away and avoid the Indians for a time.

At length, after wandering for two years, De Soto came, in 1541, to the shore of a large river. This river was wide and muddy, and had a strong current which carried much driftwood along with it. De Soto learned from the Indians that it was called Mississippi, or the "Father of Waters."

He had reached it near the spot where the city of Memphis now stands, and here his company halted and camped.

At this place the Spaniards built rafts, striking the fetters from their captives in order to use the iron for nails, and so crossed the river. They hoped in this way to escape from their savage foes; but on the other side of the river they found Indians who were just as fierce.

So the Spaniards traveled south, hoping by following the course of the river to reach the sea. This De Soto soon found to be impossible, as the country was a wilderness of tangled vines and roots, and his followers could not cross the many creeks and small rivers which flowed into the Mississippi. The horses traveled through this country with difficulty, often being up to their girths in water. Each day saw the little band grow less in numbers.

At length they returned to the banks of the river, being guided back by their horses. The men lost their way in the dreadful forest, but the instinct of the noble animals directed them aright.

Food was growing scarce, and De Soto himself was taken ill. He knew that unless something should be done soon to make the Indians help them, all would perish. So he sent word to an Indian chief saying that he was the child of the sun, and that all men obeyed him. He then declared that he wanted the chief's friendship, and ordered him to bring him food.

The chief sent back word that if De Soto would cause the river to dry up he would believe him. This, of course, De Soto could not do.

He was disappointed and discouraged at not being able to get food. The illness from which he was suffering grew worse, and he died soon afterwards.

His followers were anxious to hide his death from the natives, who were very much afraid of him. So they placed his body in the hollow of a scooped out tree, and sunk it at midnight in the water.

Those of his followers who were left decided to try to reach home by following the river to its mouth. These men were in a wretched condition. Their clothing was nearly all gone. Few of them had shoes, and many had only the skins of animals and mats made of wild vines to keep them warm. They built seven frail barks and sailed down the Mississippi, avoiding Indians all the way, and in seventeen days they came to the Gulf of Mexico.

In fifty days more they succeeded in reaching a Spanish settlement on the coast of Mexico, where they were received with much joy.

Of the gay company of six hundred and twenty who had set out with such high hopes, only three hundred and eleven men returned.

THE GREAT RIVER AMAZON, AND EL DORADO.

As you may imagine, there was great excitement and curiosity in Spain, after the voyages of Columbus, about the new lands beyond the Western Ocean.

Several of the men who had sailed with Columbus were ready to undertake new voyages of discovery. Among them was Yañez Pinzon.

The Niña.

You will remember that when Columbus made his first voyage he set out with three vessels. One of these was the *Niña.* It was commanded by Yañez Pinzon.

After Columbus had returned from his second voyage, Yañez Pinzon succeeded in fitting out a fleet to go to the New World.

In 1499 he sailed with four caravels from Palos,

the same port from which Columbus had sailed. Pinzon took with him some of the sailors who had been with Columbus, and also his three principal pilots. These pilots were men who understood how to use the astrolabe and to tell the course of the ship at sea.

Pinzon's fleet sailed toward the Canary and Cape Verde Islands, and after passing them its course was southwest across the Atlantic. At length the fleet crossed the equator, and Pinzon was the first explorer to cross the line in the western Atlantic.

The fleet sailed on for nearly five hundred miles to the southward. Here Pinzon met a terrific storm, which came very near sending his whole fleet to the bottom. He was now not far from the coast, and after the storm was over he discovered land. The land proved to be the most eastern point of South America. This was in the month of January, in the year 1500.

Pinzon and a company of his men went ashore. They did not remain long, however, as they found the Indians very hostile. The Indians attacked the Spaniards and killed several of their number. They were so furious that, after chasing the Spaniards to their boats, they waded into the sea and fought to get the oars. The Indians captured one of the rowboats, but the Spaniards at last got off to their vessels.

Pinzon then set sail and steered northward along the coast.

When his fleet came near the equator, he noticed that the water was very fresh. Accordingly he gave orders to fill the water casks of his fleet. The freshness of the water of the sea led him to sail in toward the shore.

At length he discovered whence the large volume of fresh water came. It flowed out of the mouth of a great river.

It was the mouth of the river Amazon, and so great is the volume of water which it pours into the sea that its current is noticed in the ocean two hundred miles from the shore.

This fact is not so surprising when we learn that the main mouth of this great river is fifty miles wide, that the river is four thousand miles long, including its windings, and that, besides many smaller branches, it has five tributaries, each over a thousand miles long, and one over two thousand miles long, flowing into it.

Pinzon anchored in the mouth of the river, and found the natives peaceful. In this respect they were unlike those he had met farther south. They came out to his ships in a friendly way in their canoes. But when Pinzon, a short time later, left the river, he cruelly carried off thirty-six of the Indians who had been friendly to him.

While Pinzon's fleet was in the mouth of the river, it came a second time near being wrecked.

Pinzon was, of course, in strange waters. He did not know that twice each month the tide does not rise in the usual way, but rushes up the mouth of the Amazon with great force. The tide, as a rule, is about six hours in rising and six hours in falling. In the mouth of the Amazon, however, at new moon and at full moon the tide swells to its limit in two or three minutes. It comes as a wall of water, twelve or fifteen feet high, followed by another wall of the same height. Often there is a third wall of water, and at some seasons of the year there is a fourth wall.

This peculiar rising of the tide is called the *bore.* The noise of this rushing flood can be heard five or six miles off. It comes with tremendous force, and sometimes uproots great trees along the banks. During the few days when the tide rushes up the river in this way vessels do not remain in the main channel, but anchor in coves and protected places.

Pinzon, as we have said, did not know about the sudden rising of the tide. His fleet was anchored in the main channel when the bore came, and it dashed his vessels about like toy boats and almost wrecked them.

After repairing the damage done to his fleet, he made up his mind that there was little gold to be found in those parts, and so he sailed out of the mouth of the great river, and then turned northward along the coast.

Scene on the Orinoco River.

It may be of interest to know what befell Pinzon after he left the mouth of the Amazon. We will tell you briefly.

He sailed along the coast to the northwest, and passed the mouth of the Orinoco, another large river of South America. About a hundred and fifty miles beyond the Orinoco, he entered a gulf and landed. Here he cut a large quantity of brazil wood to take back to Spain.

Then he sailed for the island of Hispaniola, now called Haiti. From this island he sailed to the Bahama Islands.

It was July when he reached the Bahamas. Misfortune again came to his fleet. While anchored in the Bahamas a hurricane came up, and two of his vessels were sunk. A third was blown out to sea. The fourth vessel rode out the storm, but the crew, thinking all the while she would sink, took to their small boats and at length reached the shore. The Indians came to them when they landed, and proved friendly.

After the hurricane was over, the vessel that had been carried out to sea drifted back. As soon as the sea was smooth enough Pinzon and his men went on board the two remaining vessels and set sail for Hispaniola.

At Hispaniola he repaired his vessels, and then sailed back to Spain. He reached Palos in September.

About three months after Pinzon sailed away from the mouth of the Amazon it was visited by a Portuguese navigator named Cabral. Although the Portuguese were not so fortunate as to discover America, yet they had been very active in making discoveries for seventy years and more before Columbus's first voyage.

In 1420 they discovered the Madeira Islands. In 1432 they discovered the Azore Islands, which lie eight hundred miles west of Portugal in the Atlantic Ocean. Their vessels, from time to time, had been pushing farther and farther down the west coast of Africa. In the middle of the century as many as fifty-one of their caravels had been to the Guinea coast, or the Gold Coast, as it was more often called. In 1484, eight years before Columbus discovered America, they had discovered the mouth of the Kongo River on the African coast.

It is not surprising, then, that their navigators were pushing out across the Atlantic soon after Columbus had led the way.

But though Cabral sailed along the whole coast of Brazil, and took possession of it in the name of the King of Portugal, he did not learn any more about the great river at the mouth of which he anchored than did Pinzon. Had he waited a few months, or had he returned to the river, he might easily have explored its course. For from July to December of each year the east wind blows steadily up the Amazon, and Cabral could have spread his sails and kept them spread as he sailed up the river for two thousand miles or more to the eastern foot of the great mountains of South America, the Andes.

The exploration of the Amazon, however, fell to

the lot of another man, Francisco Orellana by name. Orellana did not sail up the river from its mouth, but came down it from one of its sources. This was in 1540, many years, as you see, after Pinzon and Cabral had anchored at the mouth.

Orellana was one of Pizarro's men, and had been with him when the Inca of Peru was taken and afterwards put to death. It was Francisco Pizarro, as you well know, who conquered Peru. After Francisco Pizarro had conquered the country, he made his brother, Gonzalo Pizarro, governor of Quito.

This brother, while at Quito, made up his mind to cross the Andes Mountains and explore the country beyond. So he got ready an expedition, and made Orellana his lieutenant; Orellana was, therefore, second in command of the expedition.

The army was made up of three hundred and fifty Spaniards, four thousand Indians, and one thousand bloodhounds for hunting down the natives.

They had a hard march over the Andes, and suffered very much in crossing. When they were over the mountains, they discovered a river flowing toward the southeast. This was the river Napo.

Pizarro had had so hard a march across the Andes that he felt his men could not stand it to go back by the same way. He therefore encamped by the Napo River, and spent seven months in building a vessel to hold his baggage and those of his men who were ill.

He put Orellana in charge of the vessel, and ordered him to float slowly down the river while the other part of the army marched along the shore. The march was very slow and toilsome, and after a few weeks the food began to get low.

At this time Pizarro heard of a rich country farther down the stream, where the Napo flowed into a larger river. This country he wished to reach. So he sent Orellana in the vessel, with fifty soldiers, down the Napo to the larger river. There Orellana was to get food and supplies for the army and then return.

Pizarro waited and waited in vain for Orellana to return, and at last he and his men had to find their way back across the Andes with scanty food and undergo great hardships.

Orellana and the soldiers with him were carried by the current swiftly down the Napo, and in three days they came into the great river. It was indeed a great river, for the Amazon at the place where the Napo flows into it is a mile in width.

Orellana expected to find here many people and plenty of food. He found, however, only a wilderness. It was about like the country where Pizarro and his army were encamped.

Orellana could barely get food for himself and the

men with him, much less enough for Pizarro and his army. To return against the swift current would be a heavy task. After thinking the matter over, he decided to follow the great river to the sea. But he must first win the soldiers who were with him over to his plan. This he soon succeeded in doing, and they started down the Amazon.

It was no easy journey. He and the soldiers suffered greatly. But in August, 1541, after seven months of hardships, they reached the ocean, and a short time after this they sailed to Spain.

When Orellana reached Spain, he gave a glowing account of a wonderful country, rich in precious metals, through which he had passed. According to his story, it was far richer in gold than Peru.

The name El Dorado, "The Golden," was given to this fabled country; and for a score or more of years after Orellana had told his story, efforts were made to find it. Expedition after expedition set out in search of El Dorado. An explorer named Philip von Hutten, who led a party southward into the country from the northern part of South America, believed he caught sight of a city whose golden walls glistened far away in the distance. But he never reached the shining city which he thought he saw, nor was the fabled El Dorado ever found.

VERRAZZANO.

Verrazzano.

VERRAZZANO was a native of Florence, Italy, and a pirate like many other sailors of that time. Being known as a daring seaman, he was asked by Francis I., King of France, to take command of a fleet of four vessels and try to find a western passage to rich Cathay. For Francis had become very jealous of the Spaniards, and felt that his country ought to have a share in the riches of the New World.

Verrazzano sailed from France full of hope and joy; but he had gone only a short distance when a severe storm arose, and two of his vessels were lost sight of forever. The two remaining vessels were obliged to return to France.

After some delay Verrazzano started again, with one vessel called the *Dauphine.* With this vessel he reached the island of Madeira, and from this island he sailed, January 17, 1524, for the unknown world.

The voyage lasted forty-nine days, after which time a long, low coast was sighted in the distance. This coast, which was probably North Carolina, afforded no landing place, and for some time Verrazzano sailed north and then south, searching for one. The search proved unsuccessful, and as the crew were in need of fresh water, Verrazzano decided to send a boat ashore.

So a small boat was manned, and the sailors tried very hard to reach the shore, but the surf was so high that they were unable to do this. At last one brave sailor jumped from the boat into the foaming breakers and swam toward the shore. He carried in one hand presents for the Indians, who were standing at the water's edge watching the strange sight. At length the sailor succeeded in swimming so close to the shore that he was able to throw the presents to the Indians.

His courage then deserted him, and in terror he tried to swim back to his vessel. The surf, however, dashed him on the sandy beach, and he would have been drowned had not some of the Indians waded in and dragged him ashore. These Indians quickly stripped him of all his clothing and began to build an immense bonfire. The poor sailor thought his end

Indians Rescuing the Sailor.

had come, and his former companions looked on from their ship in horror at the preparations.

All of them thought that the Indians meant to burn him alive or else to cook and eat him. To their great relief, the Indians treated him very gently and kindly; they dried his clothes by the fire and warmed him.

These kind Indians looked very savage. Their skin was copper colored, their long, straight hair was tied and worn in a braid, and their faces were very stern; for, you know, an Indian never laughs or smiles.

In spite of their fierce looks, however, they were very good to the pale-faced stranger, and when he was strong again they led him back to the shore, and he swam out to his ship.

Verrazzano was glad to see his sailor return in safety from this dangerous trip. The man had risked his life, but no water had been obtained for the crew. So Verrazzano started northward, and along the coast of Maryland he made a landing and secured the much-needed fresh water.

At this place the Frenchmen had an opportunity to return the kindness that the Indians had shown their companion, but I am sorry to have to tell you that they did not do so. While searching for the water, Verrazzano and his followers came suddenly upon a little Indian boy, whom they seized and carried off to their ship. The mother of the boy came quickly from some bushes to rescue her son, and they would also have stolen her, but she made so much noise that they were obliged to run in order to escape from the rest of the tribe, who came to help her. The Frenchmen reached their ship in safety with the poor little Indian boy, and quickly set sail.

Verrazzano proceeded northward, following the shore, and at length came to a very narrow neck of water, with rising land on both sides. Through this strait Verrazzano sailed, and, to his surprise, came out into a broad and beautiful bay which was surrounded on all sides by forests, and was dotted here and there with the canoes of Indians who were coming out from the land to meet him.

You have, of course, guessed that this strait was the Narrows, which separates Staten Island from Long Island, and that the bay was the beautiful New York Bay.

Verrazzano followed the shore of Long Island to a small island, which was likely Block Island. From this island he sailed into a harbor on the mainland, probably Newport, where he remained fifteen days. Here the Indians received their pale-faced visitors with great dignity and pomp. Two of the Indian chiefs, arrayed in painted deer skins and raccoon and lynx skins, and decorated with copper ornaments, paid Verrazzano a visit of state.

Soon after this Verrazzano sailed away, again northward. The climate grew cooler and the country more rugged, and the vegetation changed. Instead of the sweet-scented cypress and bay trees which the sailors had admired along the Carolina coast, there were dark forests of stately pines, which were grand but gloomy.

Great cliffs of rock extended along the shores, and from these heights the natives looked down upon the lonely little ship in fear, anger, and amazement. At length they consented to trade with the pale-faces; but they lowered a cord from the rocks and drew up the knives, fishhooks, and pieces of steel which they demanded in exchange for furs and skins. Once Verrazzano and a few of his men tried to land. But the Indians fiercely attacked them, and a shower of arrows and the sound of the dreaded war whoop caused the Europeans to fly to their ship for safety.

So Verrazzano gave up the plan of landing among these fierce Indians, and continued his voyage northward as far as Newfoundland. Here provisions grew scarce, and Verrazzano decided to sail for home.

The return voyage was a safe one, and Verrazzano was greeted with joy when he arrived in France. Upon his discoveries the French based their claim to all the country in the New World between Carolina and Newfoundland, extending westward as far as land continued.

Verrazzano wished very much to go again to this new land and try to plant a colony and to convert the Indians to the Christian religion. But France at this time was plunged into war at home, and all trace of Verrazzano is lost. Some say that he made a second voyage, and that while exploring a wild country he was taken prisoner and killed by a savage tribe of Indians. The story that is most likely true is that he did return to the New World, and that while there he was taken prisoner by the Spaniards and hanged as a pirate.

THE FAMOUS VOYAGE OF SIR FRANCIS DRAKE—1577.

Sir Francis Drake.

UNDER the rule of Queen Elizabeth England became noted for her bold and daring seamen. These seamen were really pirates, or sea robbers; but their occupation in those days was looked upon as a lawful one by all except the people whom they plundered.

Queen Elizabeth encouraged the seafaring men to make voyages to the New World, and also to attack the Spanish ships, because she was displeased at the way the Spaniards were behaving.

The Spaniards had grown very rich and powerful by means of the wealth they had obtained in America, and in their pride they did not treat the other nations properly. They had no idea of fairness. They were selfish and wanted everything for Spain.

The English people thought that the best place to

attack the Spaniards was in the New World. They well knew that if they could cut off the supply of gold and silver which the Spanish nation was receiving from South America and the Indies, that nation would suffer.

Sir Francis Drake, a brave young knight of Elizabeth's court, formed a plan to teach the Spaniards a lesson. This plan was approved by the queen, and Drake was promised glory and riches if he should succeed in carrying it out.

In November, 1577, Drake sailed from Plymouth, England, with a fleet of five vessels and one hundred and sixty-four men. He told every one that he was going to make a voyage to Alexandria, as he did not wish the Spaniards to know that he intended to cross the Atlantic.

After a voyage of about five months, as they were sailing quietly along one evening, the crew saw strange fires in the distance. At first the sailors were alarmed; but on sailing nearer they saw that the fires were on the shore of a strange country, which Drake knew to be South America.

The natives had built these immense bonfires near the water and were preparing for some religious rites.

These natives were friendly, and Drake, after procuring some fresh supplies, sailed on, as he was in haste to reach Peru. The fleet soon entered the

Strait of Magellan, and sailed through without any mishap.

On an island in the strait they found a great number of fowl of the size of geese, which could not fly. The crew shot about three thousand of these birds, and now, having plenty of provisions, they began the journey up the west coast of South America.

The Spaniards, never dreaming that any one would have the courage to try to reach their lands by way of the Strait of Magellan, had made no attempt to defend themselves from attack from the south. They feared that their enemies might come down upon them by way of the isthmus, and strong forces had been placed there to prevent any one from crossing; but all the southern ports were defenseless.

So Drake and his men sailed up the coast, dropping in at different harbors, boldly taking everything of value that they saw, and then gayly sailing away, laughing at the surprise they left behind them.

At one place Drake found a Spanish ship laden with spoils, ready to sail to Spain. The English quickly took possession of her, set her crew ashore, and carried her out to sea. There they found that she had on board pure gold amounting to thirty-seven thousand Spanish ducats, stores of good wine, and other treasure.

At one place where they landed Drake himself

found a Spaniard lying asleep near the shore, with thirteen bars of silver by his side. The Englishmen took the silver and went quietly away, leaving the man to finish his nap.

Farther on they met a Spaniard and an Indian boy driving eight llamas, as the sheep of that country are called, toward Peru. Each llama had on its back two bags of leather, and in each bag was fifty pounds of silver. This silver Drake ordered to be placed on his ship, and then he sailed away.

Drake and the Sleeping Spaniard.

Many other places were visited in this manner, and much treasure was collected; but it was not until Drake reached Lima that the English understood the great wealth of that country. About twelve ships were in the harbor, some fully laden, and all unprotected, as the Spaniards never dreamed of attack. These ships Drake proceeded to lighten of their cargo by removing it to his own ships.

He then gave chase to another vessel, which he

heard was laden with still greater treasure. This vessel he soon found, and the cargo proved to be very valuable. Thirteen chests of plate, many tons of gold and silver, jewels, precious stones, and quantities of silk and linen were taken.

As you may suppose, after continuing this work for some time Drake's ships were very well loaded, and he and his companions began to think about returning to England. Drake felt that it would not be safe for him to return through the Strait of Magellan, as he knew the Spaniards would be expecting him. So he decided to sail across the Pacific Ocean to the Molucca Islands, and complete his journey by circumnavigating the globe.

He was at this time becalmed in the tropics, and therefore headed his ships north, hoping to find the trade wind, which would carry him across the Pacific. After proceeding north along a strange coast for nearly a month, during which time the weather gradually became colder and colder, Drake decided to enter a harbor and anchor his vessels.

The people of the country were friendly, and as the English treated them well, they remained so. They admired the brave Sir Francis Drake so much that they begged him to stay with them and be their king.

But Drake had no desire to be king over an Indian

tribe. He wanted to get back to his own good Queen Elizabeth and tell her of all the wonderful things that had happened to him. So he took possession of this country for England, and called it New Albion.

New Albion was the land which is at present known as California, and the bay in which Drake anchored is supposed to have been San Francisco Bay.

Then Drake prepared his ships for the voyage home, hoisted anchor, and was soon sailing away in the direction of the Moluccas. These islands he reached after a long voyage, and after visiting several of the Indies he proceeded across the Indian Ocean to the Cape of Good Hope and thence northward to England. He reached home in September, 1580, after an absence of three years.

How glad Queen Elizabeth was to see him! She granted him the honor of knighthood, and in other ways showed her pride in her brave subject.

Drake's ship, the *Golden Hind*, was placed in a dock at Deptford, where it stood for many years. People used to take their children to see it, and they would tell them about the *Golden Hind*, the good ship in which sailed the brave general, Sir Francis Drake, when he taught the Spaniards a lesson.

When the timber of the ship began to decay, a chair was made of some of it and given to Oxford University, where it may be seen to this day.

HENRY HUDSON.

Henry Hudson.

HENRY HUDSON was one of the best sea captains in all England. He loved the ocean, and he did not know the word "fear."

In 1607 a company of London merchants sent him to look for a northwest passage to China. These merchants knew that if such a passage could be found, the journey to China would be much shorter than by the overland route then used. It would take less time to sail around the earth near the pole than to sail around the earth near the equator. Besides, every one who had attempted to reach China by sailing west had reached, instead, that long coast of the New World, through which but one opening had ever been found. The route through this opening, the Strait of Magellan, had been proved by its discoverer, Ferdinand Magellan, to be too long for use in commerce, so traders were trying hard to find a northwest passage.

Captain Hudson proceeded northwest from England, and tried to pass between Greenland and Spitzbergen and sail across the north pole into the Pacific. Failing in this attempt, he made a second voyage, during which he tried to pass between Spitzbergen and Nova Zembla. This voyage also was unsuccessful, and Hudson returned to England. He had found no northwest passage, but he had sailed past mountains of snow and ice and had been nearer the north pole than any man had ever been before.

Captain Hudson was not discouraged by his two failures. He still believed a northwest passage could be found; and when the Dutch people asked him to make a voyage for them in search of a passage to the Pacific Ocean, he was quite willing to accept the offer.

In 1609 Hudson sailed from Amsterdam in a small craft of eighty tons, called the *Half Moon*. After sailing many days through fog and ice, the sailors refused to go farther in that direction, and then Hudson headed his ship across the Atlantic toward America. You may think it strange that Hudson should change his plans so quickly, but he knew what he was about. He had received a letter from his friend Captain John Smith, who was then in Virginia, telling him that a northwest passage was to be found along the coast of North America, north of Chesapeake Bay. This letter Hudson had in mind when he started on his voyage.

He reached Chesapeake Bay, but did not enter it, as the weather was stormy. Instead, he proceeded up the coast, looking for an opening. At length, in September, he entered a beautiful bay. Into this bay a wide river flowed which Hudson thought might be a strait that would lead into the Pacific Ocean. The water in this opening was salt, and this strengthened Hudson in the belief that it was the strait for which he had been searching so long. At the mouth of the river there was a beautiful island, long and narrow, and wooded to the shore.

The Half Moon on the Hudson River.

At first the island seemed deserted, but soon the sailors saw here and there slender curling columns of smoke rising from among the trees. This smoke showed them that the island was inhabited, and presently an Indian appeared on the shore.

This Indian looked for a moment in astonishment at the ship, and then, shouting the war whoop, bounded back into the forest. In a few minutes he reappeared, bringing other Indians with him. All were amazed at the sight of the strange ship, and they gazed in wonder and fear at it and at the white-faced, bearded strangers. Little by little, however, they lost their fear and talked with Captain Hudson. These Indians told Hudson that the name of the beautiful island was Manhattan, and that the stream led far, far to the north.

So Hudson entered the river and sailed slowly north, enjoying the charming scenery, and stopping now and then to trade and to talk with the Indians.

For twenty miles he sailed along a great wall of rock about five hundred feet high, which we now know as the Palisades. This name was given to the rocky wall because it looks like a palisade, or high fence of stakes set close together and upright in the ground.

Soon after this the river became very winding, and high mountains arose on all sides. The *Half Moon* now entered the beautiful Highlands, and her crew were the first white men to see this enchanting spot. The vessel sailed on, and at length it came to the place where the city of Hudson now stands. Here an Indian chief invited the captain to go ashore. Hudson did so, and the Indians prepared a great feast in his honor.

They gave him roast pigeons and a roast dog to eat. Hudson did not like the dog meat very much, but the Indians insisted upon cooking it for him.

Hudson Feasting with the Indians.

The Indians wanted him to stay overnight with them, and one Indian arose, and gathering together all the arrows, broke them and threw them into the fire. By this act he meant to show Hudson that he and his tribe would do him no harm.

Hudson felt that he had no time to lose, but must go on and find out whether this wonderful body of water would lead him into the Pacific. So he bade the Indians good-by and sailed away.

He went on up the river until the place was reached where Albany now stands. Here the little *Half Moon* was anchored. Indians came running down to the shore in wonder at the sight of the strange vessel. They brought with them strings of beaver skins, which they gave Hudson in exchange for pieces of gold lace, glass beads, and other trinkets. Hudson was quick to see the importance of this fur trade, and took back with him many valuable furs. Here the stream had become narrow, and was so shallow that the captain feared his vessel might run aground. He knew at last that the water was a river and not a strait, and that he was not likely to find here a passage to China. So Hudson, turning back, started down the river.

On the way down, an Indian who was in a canoe stole something from the ship. One of the crew saw the Indian commit the theft, and, picking up a gun, shot and killed him. This made the other Indians very angry, and Hudson had several fights with them.

Nevertheless the expedition reached the mouth of the river in safety, and early in October Hudson returned to Amsterdam. He had not found a northwest passage, but he had secured a large tract of country in the New World for Holland.

He told the Dutch about the rich furs to be found there, and they immediately began to build trading posts where the cities of New York and Albany now stand.

The next year Hudson made another voyage in search of a passage to Asia. This time he sailed far north into Hudson Bay. Here his crew mutinied and refused to obey him. They seized him and put him, together with his son, into an open boat, and set them adrift in the icy water.

As Hudson was never heard of again, it is supposed that he perished in the waters of the great bay which he discovered, and which still bears his name.

Eclectic School Readings

A carefully graded collection of fresh, interesting and instructive supplementary readings for young children. The books are well and copiously illustrated by the best artists, and are handsomely bound in cloth.

Folk-Story Series

Lane's Stories for Children	$0.25
Baldwin's Fairy Stories and Fables	.35
Baldwin's Old Greek Stories	.45

Famous Story Series

Baldwin's Fifty Famous Stories Retold	.35
Baldwin's Old Stories of the East	.45
Defoe's Robinson Crusoe	.50
Clarke's Arabian Nights	.60

Historical Story Series

Eggleston's Stories of Great Americans	.40
Eggleston's Stories of American Life and Adventure	.50
Guerber's Story of the Thirteen Colonies	.65
Guerber's Story of the English	.65
Guerber's Story of the Chosen People	.60
Guerber's Story of the Greeks	.60
Guerber's Story of the Romans	.60

Classical Story Series

Clarke's Story of Troy	.60
Clarke's Story of Aeneas	.45
Clarke's Story of Caesar	.45

Natural History Series

Needham's Outdoor Studies	.40
Kelly's Short Stories of Our Shy Neighbors	.50
Dana's Plants and Their Children	.65

Copies of any of these books will be sent prepaid to any address, on receipt of the price, by the Publishers:

American Book Company

New York • Cincinnati • Chicago

School Histories of the United States

McMaster's School History of the United States
By JOHN BACH MCMASTER. Cloth, 12mo, 507 pages. With maps and illustrations $1.00
Written expressly to meet the demand for a School History which should be fresh, vigorous, and interesting in style, accurate and impartial in statement, and strictly historical in treatment.

Field's Grammar School History of the United States
By L. A. FIELD. With maps and illustrations 1.00

Barnes's Primary History of the United States
For Primary Classes. Cloth, 12mo, 252 pages. With maps, illustrations, and a complete index 60

Barnes's Brief History of the United States
Revised. Cloth, 8vo, 364 pages. Richly embellished with maps and illustrations 1.00

Eclectic Primary History of the United States
By EDWARD S. ELLIS. A book for younger classes. Cloth, 12mo, 230 pages. Illustrated 50

Eclectic History of the United States
By M. E. THALHEIMER. Revised. Cloth, 12mo, 441 pages. With maps and illustrations 1.00

Eggleston's First Book in American History
By EDWARD EGGLESTON. Boards, 12mo, 203 pages. Beautifully illustrated 60

Eggleston's History of the United States and Its People
By EDWARD EGGLESTON. Cloth, 8vo, 416 pages. Fully illustrated with engravings, maps and colored plates . . 1.05

Swinton's First Lessons in Our Country's History
By WILLIAM SWINTON. Revised edition. Cloth, 12mo, 208 pages. Illustrated 48

Swinton's School History of the United States
Revised and enlarged. Cloth, 12mo, 383 pages. With new maps and illustrations 90

White's Pupils' Outline Studies in the History of the United States
By FRANCIS H. WHITE. For pupils' use in the application of laboratory and library methods to the study of United States History 30

Copies of any of the above books will be sent, prepaid, to any address on receipt of the price by the Publishers:

American Book Company

NEW YORK • CINCINNATI • CHICAGO

Supplementary Reading

JOHONNOT'S HISTORICAL READERS

SIX BOOKS. 12MO. ILLUSTRATED.

Grandfather's Stories. 140 pages	27 cents
Stories of Heroic Deeds. 150 pages	30 cents
Stories of Our Country. 207 pages	40 cents
Stories of Other Lands. 232 pages	40 cents
Stories of the Olden Time. 254 pages	54 cents
Ten Great Events in History. 264 pages	54 cents

JOHONNOT'S NATURAL HISTORY READERS

SIX BOOKS. 12MO. ILLUSTRATED.

Book of Cats and Dogs. 96 pages	17 cents
Friends in Feathers and Fur. 140 pages	30 cents
Neighbors with Wings and Fins. 229 pages . . .	40 cents
Some Curious Flyers, Creepers and Swimmers. 224 pages .	40 cents
Neighbors with Claws and Hoofs. 256 pages . . .	54 cents
Glimpses of the Animate World. 414 pages . . .	$1.00

These books are admirably adapted for use as supplementary readers. Each series contains a full course of graded lessons for reading from instructive topics, written in a style that is of the most fascinating interest to children and young people, while training them to habits of observation and storing their minds with valuable information. Each book is fully illustrated in an artistic and attractive manner.

Copies of any of the above books will be sent prepaid to any address, on receipt of the price, by the Publishers:

American Book Company

New York • Cincinnati • Chicago

The Natural Course in Music

BY

Frederic H. Ripley and Thomas Tapper

Natural Music Readers

Natural Music Primer	$0.30
Natural Music Reader, No. 1	.30
Natural Music Reader, No. 2	.35
Natural Music Reader, No. 3	.35
Natural Music Reader, No. 4	.35
Natural Music Reader, No. 5	.50
Natural Advanced Music Reader	1.00

Natural Music Charts

In seven series, A, B, C, D, E, F, and G, comprising 110 charts, substantially bound and mounted on iron tripod supporter, each series, per set 4.00

The Natural Course in Music consists of a carefully prepared series of books and charts, reasonable in price and designed to cover the whole graded course in Primary and Grammar Schools. The plan contemplates the constant use of charts, at first independent of the books, and afterwards as a systematic preparation for the lessons to be learned from day to day in the music readers.

Natural Music Series—Short Course

Book I.	For Elementary Grades	35 cents
Book II.	For Advanced Grades	40 cents

The Short Course in Music is embraced in two books and is designed for use in graded or ungraded schools in which a more complete course is deemed unnecessary or impracticable. In both books familiar and standard songs are made the basis of elementary music instruction. The Short Course embraces over 200 such songs—sacred, patriotic, occasional, and miscellaneous. Throughout, the teaching is constantly applied to the compositions of the best song writers. Exercises in two and three parts in simple form are included in the course. Few definitions are given, but a brief summary of the Elements of Music is included in an appendix. The books are illustrated by numerous portraits of authors and composers.

The books and charts of the Natural Music Course will be sent, prepaid, to any address on receipt of the price by the Publishers:

American Book Company

NEW YORK CINCINNATI CHICAGO

(22)